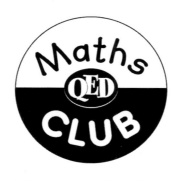

Maths QED CLUB

Adding

Ann Montague-Smith

QED Publishing

First published in the UK in 2005 by
QED Publishing
A Quarto Group company
226 City Road,
London EC1V 2TT

www.qed-publishing.co.uk

A Catalogue record for this book is available from the British Library.

ISBN 1 84538 176 9

Written by Ann Montague-Smith
Designed and edited by The Complete Works
Illustrated by Peter Lawson
Photography by Steve Lumb

Publisher Steve Evans
Creative Director Louise Morley
Editorial Manager Jean Coppendale

Printed and bound in China

With thanks to:

Contents

Counting on

Look at each of the 2 sets of cats. Find the larger set and count how many. Keep that number in your head and count on for the smaller set. What number do you get to?

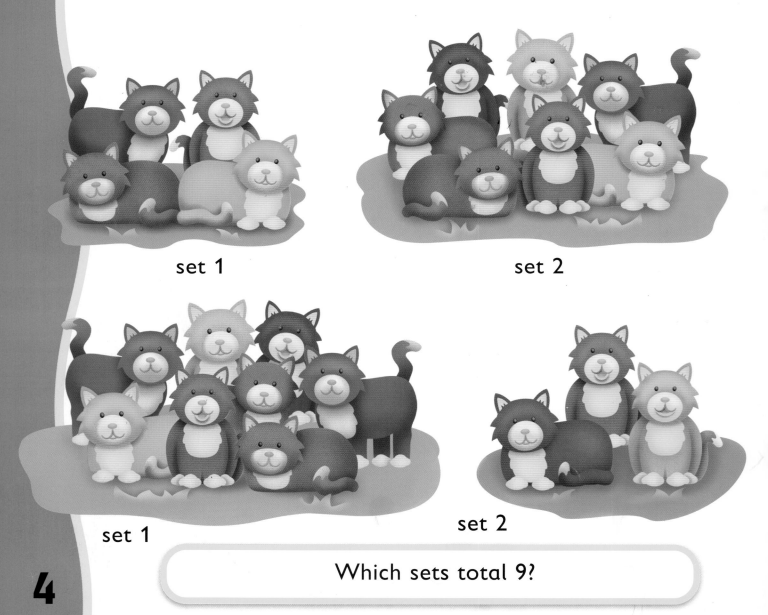

set 1

set 2

set 1

set 2

Which sets total 9?

set 1

set 2

Challenge

You will need 9 counters. How many different ways can you find to make 2 sets which total 9? Write some addition sentences using + and = to show what you have found.

1+8=9

set 1

set 2

set 1

set 2

5

Adding small numbers

Which 2 sets add up to 8? Find out by counting on in ones from the larger number. How many different ways can you find to do this?

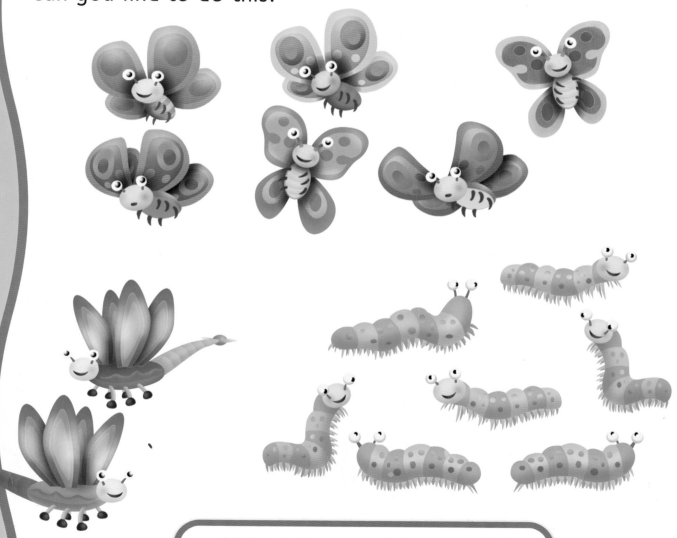

Which 3 sets add up to 12?
Find 3 different ways to do this.

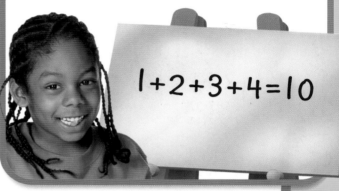

Now try this

Add 4 sets together.
What different totals can you make?
Write them as addition sentences.
Use + and = like this.

$1+2+3+4=10$

7

Totals of 10

Find 2 sets which total 10.

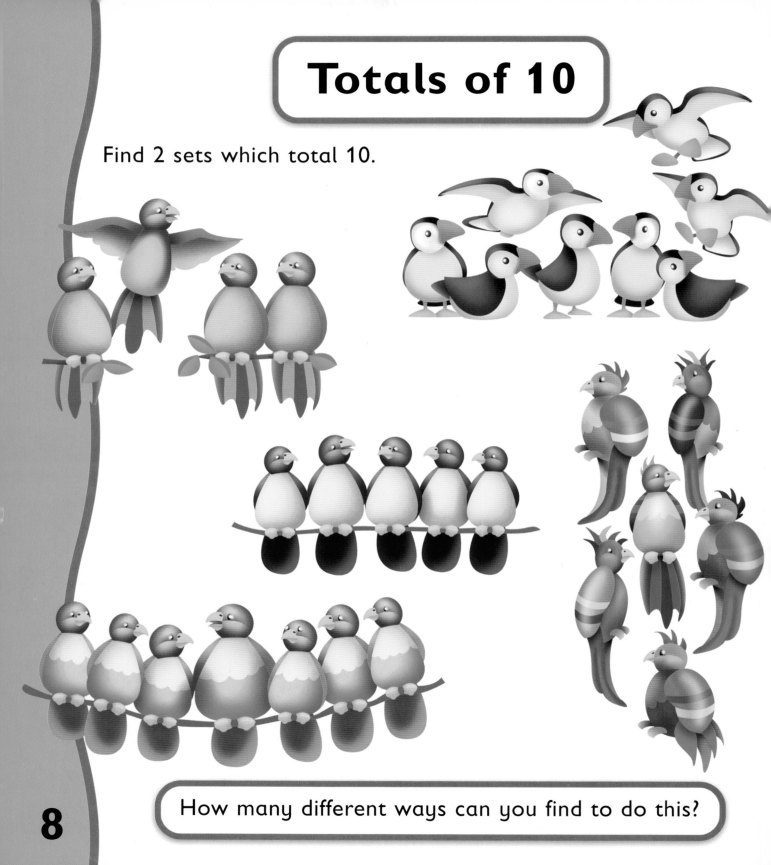

How many different ways can you find to do this?

Now try this

You will need 10 counters and a friend.

Take some of the counters.

Don't tell your friend how many you have.

Now ask your friend to look at what is left.

Can he/she say how many you took?

Now swap over.

Adding to 10

Play this game with a friend. You will need some counters in two colours. Take turns to choose a number from both circle 1 and circle 2. Add the numbers together. Cover your answer on the bears' picnic blanket with a counter. The winner is the one with the most counters on the blanket.

circle 1

1 2
3 4

circle 2

6 1 2
5 4 3

10
2
3
1
6
1
3
2

Play again, but this time choose 2 numbers each time from the picnic blanket which you think total 10. Cover both numbers with counters if you are correct.

11

Doubles and near doubles

Play this game with a friend. You will need a 1–6 dice and two counters. Take turns to throw the dice. Move that number on the track. Work out the answer to the addition sentence. If you get it wrong, move your counter back to where you were. The winner is the first one to the finish.

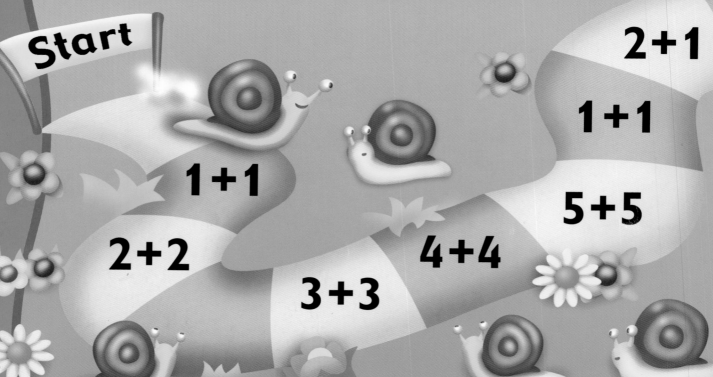

Start

2+1

1+1

1+1

5+5

2+2

4+4

3+3

Try these strategies. For doubles, count on in ones like this, 4 and 5, 6, 7, 8. For near doubles, double and add 1 like this, 4+4+1.

12

1+2

3+2

6+6

4+3

2+3

Now try this

Use the numbers 6, 7, 8, 9 and 10.
Double them. Now can you find near
doubles such as 6+7, 7+8 and 8+9?
Write some addition sentences for
your doubles and near doubles.

6+6=
7+8=

Finish

3+4

5+4

6+5

4+5

5+6

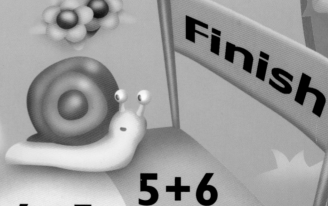

13

Using 5

You will need some counters and a coin. Throw the coin onto the spinner. Split the spinner number into 5 and a bit. So 9 would be 5+4. Now add 5 to 5+4. Cover your answer on one of the stars with a counter.

spinner

6 7
8 9

11

13

12

14

Throw the coin 5 more times.
Can you do these additions really quickly now?

12

13

14

14

11

15

Now try this

Take turns with a friend.
Throw the coin onto the spinner twice.
Make two '5 and a bit' numbers.
Can you see how to add them? The first
one to have 5 correct answers wins!

7+6= 5+2+5+1= 10+3=13

Adding 9 and 11

There is a trick you can use when adding 9. For example, take 6+9. Think of 6+10. Now take away 1. These dogs have some bones. They have hidden 9 more. How many bones has each dog in total?

Suppose the dogs had hidden 11 bones. Try +10 then +1. How many bones has each dog now?

Challenge

The dogs have hidden 8 bones this time. Think about how you could work this out by adding 10. What would you need to take away?

Where have I buried my bones?

Adding teen numbers

Look at the numbers on each tile. Find the total of each pair of tiles. Remember, if you know that 5+4=9 then you can work out that 15+4=19.

12 **3**

15 **4**

16 **2**

17 **1**

Add 1 to each tile. What is the total of each pair now?

Challenge

Write down these addition sentences. 10+4= 11+4= 12+4= Can you work out the answers? What would the next sentence be? And the next one? Tell an adult about the patterns you can see.

19

An addition problem

Here are some boxes of toys. Each box shows you how many toys are inside. Supposing you wanted 15 toys. Which boxes would you choose?

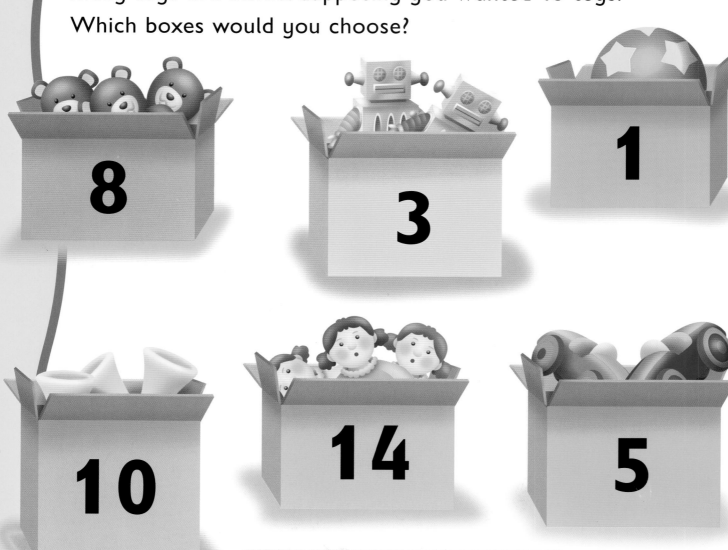

8

3

1

10

14

5

How many different ways can you find to choose 15 toys?

Challenge

Find different ways to choose 20 toys. Write an addition sentence each time.

11+9=20

21

Supporting notes

Counting on – pages 4-5

Putting the larger set first and counting on for the second set is a very useful mental strategy. Ask the children to count on in ones. They may find it helpful to keep a check by using their fingers, so that they count on for the correct amount. For example, 6+3 is 6 and 7, 8, 9. The children put up three fingers, one at a time, to keep a check of their count.

Adding small numbers – pages 6-7

Encourage the children to count on in ones from the larger number. For example, for 5+6 say 6 and 7, 8, 9, 10, 11. So 5+6 is 11. The children can keep track of the mental count using their fingers. Encourage the children to write an addition sentence using + and =.

Totals of 10 – pages 8-9

The children will find it helpful to use their fingers at first. Say, 'I'll say a number. You show me with your fingers how many more I will need to make 10.' The children can then use their 10 digits to find the answer.

Adding to 10 – pages 10-11

The children will need to have rapid recall of all addition facts to at least 5+5, and then begin to know all addition facts to 10+10. Encourage them to use strategies, such as 'Put the larger number in your head and count on in ones,' where they do not have rapid recall of the fact.

Doubles and near doubles — pages 12-13

The children will find the strategy of counting on from one of the numbers helpful. Where it is a near double, suggest that they count on from the smaller number and add 1. Some children may prefer to count on from the larger number and subtract 1. This is also a good strategy.

Using 5 — pages 14-15

Discuss the partitioning strategy with the children. Take 5+8. This is the same as 5+5+3 or 10+3. If the children are beginning to understand about place value, then they will not need to add the 3 to the 10, instead they will see that 10+3=13, because the '3' moves directly to the units place.

Adding 9 and 11 — pages 16-17

Understanding place value will help the children to see that if 10 is added to any number, then it leaves the units unchanged. For example, 6+10 is 16. If the children are unsure, use a number line at first so that they can count on 10, then add/subtract 1 to complete the calculation.

Adding teen numbers — pages 18-19

Encourage the children to use what they already know, or can calculate mentally, in order to work out what they do not know. If the children are unclear about moving from, for example, 5+3=8 to 15+3=18, then use a number line and show them how this is the same as 10+5+3.

An addition problem — pages 20-21

The children may find it helpful to write the numbers on the boxes of toys on to some pieces of paper. Then ask them to try different combinations of their boxes of toys to find totals of 15. Some children may find a number line from 0 to 20 useful as an aid to calculating. They can count along the line. However, do encourage mental counting in order to find totals.

Using this book

The illustrations in this book are bright, cheerful and colourful, and are designed to capture children's interest. Sit somewhere comfortable together as you look at the book. Children of this age will usually need to have the instructional words on the pages read to them. Please read these to them, then encourage them to take part in the activity.

In this book children are encouraged to work both practically, by counting pictures on the pages, and mentally, by counting 'in their heads'. The range of totals for adding extends from up to 10, then up to 20. Children are encouraged to use strategies of counting on from the larger number in ones; finding two 5s to make a 10 and adding on, such as $5+6=5+5+1=10+1$; and extending this to adding on 10 and adjusting by 1, such as in $9+5=10+5-1$; learning double facts to $5+5$, then deriving near doubles from this such as $4+5=4+4+1$ or $5+5-1$. For strategies that involve adding beyond 10, children will find it most useful to understand about place value; that is, that for any teen number, for example 13, the 1 stands for '10' and the 3 for '3 units.'

For some children, modelling addition on a number line can help. Either draw a 0–10 or 0–20 number line, or use a simple ruler, with just centimetres marked on it, up to 20. Then children can use the ruler to model the addition sentence.

Some of the activities in this book are games for two or more to play together. Play the game and make some 'deliberate' mistakes. This will challenge the children to spot the mistake and to correct you. This will help you to assess how well they understand and can use the mathematical idea which the pages are teaching.

Remember, learning about mathematics should always be a positive experience. So, enjoy the mathematical games, activities and challenges in this book together!